CITY OF GARDENS

Victoria

ELMA SCHEMENAUER

THE EMPRESS

Published by Weigl Educational Publishers Limited
6325 – 10 Street SE
Calgary, Alberta, Canada
T2H 2Z9
Web site: http://www.weigl.com

Canadian Cataloguing in Publication Data
Schemenauer, Elma.
 Ottawa

  (Canadian Cities)
  Includes Index
  ISBN 1-896990-53-3

  1. Victoria (B.C.)--Juvenile literature. I. Title. II. Series:
Canadian Cities (Calgary, Alta)
FC3846.33.S34 2000   j971.1'28   C00-910626-X
F1089.5.V6S34 2000

Printed and bound in Canada
1 2 3 4 5 6 7 8 9 0   04 03 02 01 00

Project Coordinator
Jill Foran
Design
Warren Clark
Cover Design
Terry Paulhus
Copy Editors
Heather Kissock, Bryan Pezzi
Layout
Lucinda Cage

Photograph Credits
Every reasonable effort has been made to trace ownership and to obtain permission to reprint copyright material.
The publishers would be pleased to have any errors or omissions brought to their attention so that they may be
corrected in subsequent printings.

Archive Photos: page 11T-R (Munawar Hosain); British Columbia Archives: pages 6M-L, 6B-L, 7M, 7B-R, 8T-L, 8B,
10T-R, 10B-L, 11B; Cheadle Photography Inc.: cover, pages 4B-R, 5T-L, 5B-L, 9T-R, 9M-L, 9B-L, 12T-L, 12M-R, 13T,
13B, 15B-R, 16B, 17T-R, 17B-L, 18T-L, 18M, 19T, 20B, 21T-R, 22, 23R, 24T-R, 25T-R, 25M-L, 25B-R, 27T-R, 27B,
28T-R, 28B-L 29T-L; Corbis: page 21B; Corel Corporation: pages 1, 5B-R, 12B-R, 20T-L, 23L, 26B, 29B-R, 30M, 30B;
Martha Jones: pages 3T-L, 3B, 14T-R, 18B-L; Royal British Columbia Museum: pages 3T-R, 24B-L; Silken & Co.:
page 11M-L.

Contents

Introduction

Victoria is British Columbia's capital city. Located at the south end of Vancouver Island, Victoria has a distinctively British mood and style. The city is known for the whales, seals, and dolphins that swim in its ocean waters. It is also known for its many gardens.

Victoria

Canada

0   500 km

Getting There

You can fly to Victoria from certain North American cities. If you are on a **float plane**, you will land in Victoria's Inner Harbour. All other planes land at Victoria International Airport.

You can also take a ferry to Victoria. Ferries run from the B.C. mainland and from some American cities.

At a Glance

Climate

In the summer, Victoria is a sunny place. Even with its many hours of sunshine, summer days stay cool. This is because of the cooling waters surrounding the city. Average daytime temperatures in July are only about 20° Celsius.

Victoria winters are cloudy and damp. Rain can fall almost every other day. Snow and ice are unusual in the city, since temperatures rarely drop below freezing. The average temperature in January is about 7° Celsius. Victoria has the most gentle climate in Canada. While people in colder regions of Canada play hockey on frozen ponds, Victorians play soccer in green fields.

Area & Population

When people speak of Victoria, they usually include the **urban** areas around it. Among these are Oak Bay, Esquimalt, View Royal, and Saanich. This whole urban region has about 330,000 people. Of these, about 74,000 live in the city of Victoria itself.

Blossom Counting in Garden City

Spring comes early in Victoria, and people like to celebrate its early arrival by counting all of the flowers in the city. Victoria's blossom count is an annual event. Each year, the city's chamber of commerce asks people to go out into their gardens and count the daffodils, crocuses, and other flowers. People phone the numbers in to local radio stations. The stations add them up and send the totals across the country. According to Victoria meteorologist Rick Lee, "One year four billion flowers were in bloom."

Interesting Statistics

1. Victoria and its surrounding urban region have an area of about 2,000 square kilometres.

2. Flying from Vancouver to Victoria takes fifteen to thirty minutes.

3. Riding a ferry from Vancouver to Victoria takes about an hour and forty minutes.

4. Victoria is about 75 kilometres southwest of the B.C. mainland.

5. Victoria's latitude is as far north as Anacortes in the nearby state of Washington.

The Past

Early Settlement

Aboriginal peoples were the first to settle in what is now Victoria. Among them were the Songhee and Kosapsom. These peoples belonged to a group of Aboriginal nations known as the **Coast Salish.** They lived in cedar houses, fished for salmon, and hunted sea otters for their soft brown fur.

In 1842, a fur trader named James Douglas arrived. He was a leader of the Hudson's Bay Company. This company, based in Britain, was the main fur trading company in what is now Canada.

In 1843, Douglas and his men built Fort Victoria, naming it for the British queen. They hired Songhee people to cut long wooden stakes for the walls around the fort. After it was built, settlers came from Britain. They began growing wheat on the plains around the fort. Elsewhere on Vancouver Island, British and other settlers were fishing, trading furs, logging, and mining coal. Fort Victoria and the settlement around it became their main town.

In 1858, thousands of gold seekers began passing through the Fort Victoria settlement. They were heading for the B.C. mainland because rich gold fields had been found there. For several years, miners kept passing through Victoria. The streams of miners made the settlement grow. Business people arrived to build hotels, rent rooms, and sell goods to the gold seekers. By 1862, Victoria was so big that it was officially made a city.

Fort Victoria grew as miners and business people came to set up permanent homes.

Key Events

1843 James Douglas builds Fort Victoria.

1858 Miners start passing through the Fort Victoria settlement. A police force is set up.

1862 Victoria becomes a city.

1865 The British Royal Navy sets up its main Pacific naval base at Esquimalt.

Studying in Victoria

The British Columbia Archives and Records office offers access to public records for people who are conducting historical research. It is also a great place to research your family roots.

Victoria is home to two colleges. Camosun College is a community college. It offers a range of programs. They include nursing, engineering, computer science, tourism, accounting, and business. Lester B. Pearson College offers a two-year college program for gifted students from around the world. There are also two universities in Victoria. Royal Roads University and the University of Victoria provide students with excellent learning opportunities.

At the University of Victoria, some students study whales at their Whale

Many people in Victoria are trying to find ways to study whales without harming them or their environment.

Research Lab. These students are trying to find ways people can enjoy watching the huge sea creatures without harming them or their environment. Another Victoria-area site for studying sea creatures and their environment is the Institute of Ocean Sciences. Run by the Canadian government, it is one of nine ocean sciences sites across Canada.

Royal Roads University and the University of Victoria provide students with excellent learning opportunities.

Sports and Recreation

Water and Wildlife

The Victoria area is home to many beautiful parks. One is Beacon Hill Park in downtown Victoria. It has a petting zoo, duck ponds, waterfront walks, and pebble beaches. When the wind is right, Beacon Hill Park is a good place to fly kites. The Kinsmen Gorge Park in Esquimalt has playgrounds, beaches, picnic tables, tennis courts, and trails. Uplands Park in Oak Bay offers hiking, bird-watching, and spring flower viewing.

Victoria is a great place to take part in water sports. Activities include sailing, scuba diving, fishing, and boating. While you are out on the water, you may see seals, sea lions, bald eagles, and great blue herons. You may also see different kinds of whales.

Victoria is the perfect place for water sports.

The petting zoo at Beacon Hill Park is a popular destination for animal lovers.

Team Sports

Only the brave swim in the ocean around Victoria. The ocean water is very cold. Most people swim in pools or lakes instead. Lakes in the Victoria area include Prospect Lake, Beaver Lake, and Elk Lake. Elk Lake is a training centre for the Canadian rowing team.

The Victoria Cougars used to be a team in the National Hockey League. They won the Stanley Cup in 1925. The Cougars are no longer part of the NHL, but there are two younger teams that carry their name. The Bantam Cougars and the PeeWee Cougars play other teams around Victoria Island.

The Canadian rowing team trains in the Victoria area.

Lacrosse is another popular team sport in Victoria. Lacrosse is fast-paced and exciting. Each player has a curved stick with a pocket of netting. Teams use their sticks to try to toss a hard rubber ball into each other's goals. The Victoria Shamrocks play lacrosse in Memorial Arena.

History of Lacrosse

Lacrosse comes from a game called "baggattaway." This game was invented by Aboriginal people in Eastern Canada. In 1638, a missionary named Jean de Brebeuf saw the game being played, and called it "la crosse" because the stick the players used

looked like a bishop's cross. By the 1880s, lacrosse was the most popular sport in Canada. Today, the sport is played mostly in Ontario and British Columbia.

Tourism

The B.C. Parliament Buildings

Vancouver Island is named for Captain George Vancouver. He explored the B.C. coast in the 1790s. Today, George Vancouver's gold-coloured statue stands on top of B.C.'s Parliament Buildings. It gazes out over Victoria's beautiful Inner Harbour.

Victoria's Parliament Buildings are a popular attraction. Their rounded copper domes have turned a lovely green with time. At night, the buildings are outlined by sparkling white lights. The Knowledge Totem stands in front of the Parliament Buildings. It

The grounds of the Parliament Buildings are dotted with statues and monuments honouring important historical figures.

symbolizes the stories passed down by B.C.'s Aboriginal nations. Statues and monuments are scattered around the grounds of the buildings. A statue of Queen Victoria serves to remind people of the queen for whom the city was named. A marble pillar stands as a reminder of James Douglas, the man who built Fort Victoria.

Butchart Gardens

There are many gardens around Victoria. Flowers bloom everywhere, even on the city's lamp-posts. Perhaps the most popular gardens in the Victoria area are the Butchart Gardens. Jenny Butchart started them in 1904. Her husband, Robert Pim Butchart, and his company had dug out a huge area of **limestone** to make cement. Jenny thought that the **quarry** they left behind looked bare and ugly. She began planting flowers and trees. She hired people to help her, and soon the gardens became famous.

Today, you can stroll through the lovely gardens Jenny started. There are four. They are the Sunken, Rose, Japanese, and Italian Gardens. On some summer evenings, fireworks crackle through the sky above the gardens.

People from all over the world come to see the Butchart Gardens.

The Crystal Garden

The Crystal Garden is another great place to visit. It is a huge glass building that houses tropical plants and animals. Flamingos, wallabies, monkeys, and butterflies are among the wildlife that live in the jungle setting of the Crystal Garden.

At the Butchart Gardens, each of the four gardens has its own theme.